A II U

NEXT

To Pam,

I hope you enjoy
the book & it makes
you laugh!

Julie

11/3/12

And So I Say
NEXT

When Frogs Turn Out to Be Toads, Throw Them Back in the ^Dating Pond!

J. PHILIPPONE

TATE PUBLISHING
AND ENTERPRISES, LLC

Published by Tate Publishing & Enterprises, LLC
127 E. Trade Center Terrace | Mustang, Oklahoma 73064 USA
1.888.361.9473 | www.tatepublishing.com

Tate Publishing is committed to excellence in the publishing industry. The company reflects the philosophy established by the founders, based on Psalm 68:11,
"The Lord gave the word and great was the company of those who published it."

Book design copyright © 2012 by Tate Publishing, LLC. All rights reserved.
Cover design by Jan Sunday Quilaquil
Interior design by Lauro Talibong

Published in the United States of America

ISBN: 978-1-62024-832-4
HUMOR / Topic / Relationships
FAMILY & RELATIONSHIPS / Love & Romance
12.08.13

Acknowledgments

Grateful acknowledgement goes to my family and friends for supporting me through all these crazy experiences, especially my mom and dad, who had nothing but encouraging words every time I finished a chapter and read it to them.

A Word from Julie's Pastor

Hilarious! Let us remember these lessons from Julie so we do not need to take ten years to learn "*to trust in the Lord in all things and He will direct our paths.*" God can direct us, not only give us discernment. He will give us the desires of our heart when our desires match His. We can learn from experience or we can pray, wait, and listen to God.

Julie has the Best Man in her life that anyone could have, and I have told her unless a man has a handwritten note from Jesus—stay away!

Ron Lenahan, Pastor
Faith to Faith Fellowship
"*A Christ Centered Church*"

Contents

Preface

Every morning, I talk with my mother. She always asks me how my current relationship is going and if they are at the "curb" yet. It was a private joke we shared. Trash day is Thursdays at my house. We would both laugh, and she would chime in with her special brand of humor: "Next." Thus, the title of this book.

Introduction

Here I am, sitting in the Atlanta airport in the month of June, waiting for my connecting flight to Florida. The airport is hustling, but my little space I have chosen to sit at is peaceful. It is giving me time to reflect over the last few years of dating. The inner peace is allowing me to hear God and the Holy Spirit just as loud as they can be, urging me to write this book, over which I have been procrastinating for the last few years.

People wonder why we go through difficult periods in our lives. There were so many crazy dates. It was definitely a sign from above. For me, I now know that without a doubt I am supposed to share my experience with others. Even if I reach only one person, in writing this book, I have done what God wants me to do.

I sit here, watching the people running for their connections and others strolling and taking in the sights of the airport, pondering the last few years of my life. I see the different couples passing by. I observed older couples settled comfortably in their relationships, holding hands at eighty or so years old. The newlyweds with that fire-in-the-night passion in their eyes locked on each other as if no one else was around. The look she gave him was one of a sparkle in her eye and a come-hither smile of love as he reciprocated with that look that says, "I love you and I want to make love to you here and now."

How wonderful that feeling of euphoria is in the beginning of a relationship. Unfortunately, at present, people do not work at keeping relationships alive, and they look to the next relationship to find what is missing without even giving much thought to the consequences. It has become socially acceptable to just get a divorce. I hear people say, "Yes. This is my practice marriage," or, "Yes. This is my *first* wife," clearly meaning that divorce is inevitable. What an unbelievable state we are in because of instant gratification and lack of desire to put some work into the relationship. It is so important to let God guide you in choosing your mate so you can be blessed with all that He wants for your life by doing things justly and in order of God's will and not of our own.

I believe the following chapters will help enlighten someone who needs to hear about my dating life experiences or just help them acknowledge, *Wow! I am glad I never had to go through what Julie did*, and recognize how blessed they are in their lives. And for those women who have traveled these crazy dating roads with me, it will provide a laugh. The names have been changed to protect the toads out there whom I have encountered, but the events are real.

Where do I begin?

The Divorce

It started in the late eighties during Memorial Day weekend. We met at a popular disco. It was all there, the big hair, the tight clothes, the lit dance floor, complete with the sound of the Bee Gee's playing loudly in the background.

We were young, thin, beautiful, and tan. I was drawn to him from across the dance floor. He had the Italian macho look mastered. He was wearing a heavily starched white shirt with a thick gold chain adorning him. Like all good Italian Catholic boys, the chain had a gold cross hanging from it. He was chewing gum (always!) and had on stonewashed blue jeans with an athletic cut to fit his body-builder legs. Snakeskin boots finished out the look.

He was a well-built man of five feet nine inches tall with soap opera good looks. His body-builder massive legs were the size of two of mine put together. He always strutted with his signature look, never a hair out of place. He was proud of the fact that he had Elvis hair, I later found out. After getting to know him, my mother affectionately called him "the peacock."

He was standing with his friends when I recognized one of them. It was a guy who had dated my cousin. Sensing my opportunity for a natural introduction, I slowly sauntered over in my three-inch heels (as I am only five feet three inches tall, looking to be taller) and new all-white lace outfit. And I had not forgotten to discretely wear the scent of the year, Charlie! At last, I had found my excuse to meet the hunk who captured my attentions. His name was Lou.

We chatted and connected instantly. It was as if we had known each other for years. At the end of the evening, we ended up out for breakfast at a local restaurant. When we walked in, there was my ex-fiancé, standing in the doorway. The reason we broke up was because he cheated on me and I wanted nothing more to do with him. Lou went to tell the hostess we needed a table. It was then when my ex took me by the arm and tried to plead his case for me to come back to him. When I told Lou about him and the situation, he tried to protect me. He grabbed my ex by the arm and escorted him out to the parking lot. I have to admit that his willing-ness to protect my honor made me instantly fall in love with him. I thought I had found my knight in shining armor rid-ing to my rescue on a gleaming white horse. Instead, it was a maroon Buick Riviera and not a white horse.

I tried to be the perfect wife. I made him breakfast, packed his lunches, and cleaned his clothes. Conversely, if he wanted a new car, we got one. If he wanted a new suit, he got one.

If he wanted a new place to live, we moved. What we had or acquired was never enough.

After we had been married for almost ten years, it became clear to me that it was time to leave. How do we know *if* we should leave a marriage when it *is* time to leave? My very close friend Jesse said to me "You don't know until you know." If someone tells you when to leave, then you tend to blame them for their advice. You can continue to ask enough people until you get the answer you are looking for and then use it for the basis from which you to make your decision. Or you can read the signs and follow your heart.

So I went home to my ex, or should I say "Y." I frustratingly said, "You exhaust me. I have gained weight and lost my hair. I have two jobs to support us, and all you do is go to the gym, continue to look good, and are *still* deciding what to do as a career." I continued emphatically, "I need some time away. I am planning to leave Friday with our daughter to spend time at my mother's."

His response was overwhelmingly shocking. He actually said, "Could you wait until Monday? I don't have anything to do this weekend."

Well, I guess that answered that question. You know when you are making the right decision because you will have that feeling of perfect peace coming over your whole being. That was exactly how I felt at that moment.

Out of consideration for the "Y" and for my daughter's sake and nothing else, I need not go into great detail about all that transpired with Lou. There are many more stories I could tell, but I think you get the gist. I simply want to highlight for women (or men) an important point that we should not be blind to in a relationship. Some tendencies people reveal in the beginning might initially appeal to you, but you need to look *years* down the line and ask yourself: *Is this going to annoy me a week, year, or a decade from now?*

What I did *not* know was that his actions in the eighties were going to be the reasons for the end of our marriage in the new millennium. I found out that if people show arrogance and possessiveness, they are insecure. His fears actually forced the end of our relationship.

But every toad has a silver lining. Let me conclude by saying he *did* try in his own way to be a good husband through the years we were married and is very attentive to our daughter. In one singular way, I am grateful for Lou, because I would have never been blessed with my sweet baby girl, who is now heading to college soon. I am sure that adventure will be another whole book.

Lesson Learned

No matter how much you love someone or do things for them, the fact is people don't change unless they want to. My friend's husband has a saying, and *how true* it is: "*You can lead a horse to water, but sometimes they just want Jack Daniels!*" When people show you unwittingly who they are, *believe* them and move on if it is not healthy.

And so I say, *"Next!"*

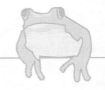

The Transition Person

At the end of any relationship (or marriage, especially), there is usually what I believe to be a "transition person." This person does exactly what the label sounds like: transitions you through from the old relationship and into another one.

If you stay with the transition person, you are usually in for trouble. Your mind is still clouded from the recent breakup. People will usually find the extreme opposite of their ex, but in reality, they might even be ten times worse off than the situation they just left.

I will illustrate my point in the retelling of the experience I had with Geno. He and I had known each other all through my marriage. We both were in family businesses and related well with each other. He was much younger than me, but once I left my husband, Geno asked me out. I accepted the invitation, as he was someone who was very intelligent and always kind and understanding. Most importantly, he was good to my daughter when we would visit his business.

For our first date, he showed up with a box of cannolis and tickets to a monster truck show. Yes, you read that correctly.

Some women might have been insulted, but what I can say about myself is that I am a bit of a gear head and I thought it was a great idea. Things soon flourished, and we became closer. He seemed too good to be true. Guess what. *When you think someone is too good to be true, they likely are!*

As for the next series of events, I would have never imagined them in my wildest dreams. On visiting his home, I found that Geno apparently had a small weapon collection, which he proceeded to show me. Let me expand on the contents of his arsenal: a grenade launcher (complete with live grenades, one of which he held in his hand, pulled the pin out, and put in front of me—talk about a heart-stopping experience!), not one but two 9-mm semiautomatic handguns, a .38 and .45 Smith & Wesson revolver, a sawed-off shot gun, and a six-foot gun safe filled to the brim with ammunition.

I asked if these guns were registered, and he told me in the infinite macho Italian way, "Never you mind, honey." I decided I would keep an open mind.

Do you think I am crazy? Well, I'll admit, I wasn't in my right mind. I was reeling from the divorce and struggling with some low self-esteem. Against my better judgment, I decided to stick around.

Attempting to make the best of it, and so I would not be intimidated, I had him take me to the gun range. I learned how to load a clip of ammunition and insert it into the Smith & Wesson .45-caliber gun. When I began to target practice, something I was not expecting happened.

Tears began rolling down my face, my hands were shaking, and my soul was *screaming*. I immediately had to stop. As a Christian woman, the thoughts of what I was doing violently overwhelmed me. The prospect of having the power of life and death in my hands was too much for me to bear.

After that incident, I started noticing other things, such as his tendency toward anger and rage. We were in a restaurant one day, someone bumped into him, and I could see the rage come to his face. The same thing happened at the movie theater, and I just prayed that he did not take the gun out to settle it. These emerging characteristics (along with all the guns) caused me to become concerned. When I shared my concerns with Geno, it did not go well at all. He was not happy with my questions about his anger or his guns. I decided that I needed to end it, and I felt that if I did not get out right away, it would be worse later. I told him that sometimes people are just in our lives for "just a season" and that maybe our "season" was over. He did not like that. He grabbed me and, with a hold that would kill a small child, forced a kiss on me. Now afraid for myself, my heart began to race, and I began quietly in my mind praying to God to give me the right words to make him let me go. When he finally did, I asked him to give me some space for a few days and then we could talk. He hesitantly agreed, but that was far from the end of Geno.

A while later, we talked on the phone. He told me he would get help and asked me to go to counseling with him.

The counseling was going well—or so I thought. It took an unanticipated turn for the worst because it had brought up so many memories and family issues. He could not deal very well with all the problems that surfaced and broke down. His family blamed me for his breakdown, of course, and forbade him to see me again. I was relieved to assume that this was finally the end of our troubled relationship.

After a few months, the phone calls started up, and he told me he wanted me back. That was not a possibility, as by that time, I was genuinely afraid of him. To get away from him, I moved, changed jobs, and secured a new home phone number, but he found me. My last encounter was at the grocery store near my new apartment.

He was waiting there and was watching for me. He got out of his truck and approached me with determination in his eyes. I could feel every muscle in my body tensing to brace myself for what might happen next. He said he would come back for me when his life was in better order, and right in the middle of the parking lot, I demanded, "Would that be of my own free will or at *gun*point?" He looked shocked that I would even ask such a thing. Geno got in his truck and left, screeching his tires. I immediately went home and filed a police report. They said that unless he harmed me, they could do nothing further. Nice country, America; unless you're harmed bodily, the police cannot help you.

God, as my protector, I have not heard from him in years.

Lesson Learned

A big red flag was anger issues, and ask how many guns they own *and* if they are they *registered*. Then run—don't walk the other the way!

And so I say, "Next!"

A Blast from the Past

What can I say about my first love from high school? Like Romeo and Juliet, as teenagers, we were forbidden to see each other because he was the bad boy whom every good girl loved. He had the muscle car and the feathered-back hair. He looked like the kid from the movie *The Breakfast Club*, the one who tore through the school, causing trouble. But in spite of being off limits, as a teenager, I would sneak out of the house in the middle of night to drive to the beach with Romeo and watch the sunrise. I would think dreamily, *How romantic. We will be together forever!*

When I was fifteen, my mother and father forbade me to see him again. I did not cross paths with Romeo again until I was eighteen. It was just as exciting and full of trouble as the first time we stole time together. We pledged our love to each other again, but that time it only lasted a month, and he was gone again.

Guess what. He showed up again briefly when I was twenty-two, just before I met my ex-husband. The same exciting but predictable scenario: love, excitement, and then gone again. I thought that surely that would be the end of it.

When I first divorced, I moved into my parents' condo. There was a man across the street with whom I became friends right away, and periodically, he would come over and help me move things. One of those times I asked him to give me a hand, I had a box I needed from the garage and could not reach it. As he was bringing the box down from the rafters, a bunch of old letters fell out. They were the love notes I had kept from Romeo all these years. I forgot I had them. My neighbor was so intrigued, and I found myself reading them to him. As I was sharing my cache, it was obvious that he could see the smile on my face and hear the excitement in my voice, even after all those years. He asked me with intrigue what Romeo's last name was and went home.

Two weeks later, my neighbor came over and handed me a slip of paper. On it was Romeo's phone number. I was shocked. It turned out that he worked with my neighbor. Small world—no degree of separation. You guessed it. We started up all over again.

He told me he was going through a divorce and that he would love to spend time with me again. He professed his never-ending love for me, and I to him again. Well, I do not know why, but I thought for sure *that time* our relationship was going to work.

We spent time together listening to Led Zeppelin like we used to and danced the nights away, reliving our teen years and some great memories. Unfortunately, it was short-lived,

J. Philippone

again. I think we all have someone like this in our lives. Why is it so tough to let them go?

Here's what forced the end this time: a month into the renewed relationship, he called me one night and told me he needed me to pick him up at a bar. It was a Wednesday. He knew my schedule with my daughter. She would be with her dad Wednesday, Friday, and Sunday that week, and he remembered it.

I did as he asked. When I arrived, he couldn't walk. I helped him to the car and let him come to my condominium. In horror, I watched as he sat at my dining room table and snorted a sleeping pill up his nose. *Really!* In absolute disbelief, I asked what he was doing. He told me that he snorted it because it gets into his system quicker. *Do I look like I just fell off the turnip truck?* Romeo passed out on the couch. He raised the roof and shook the walls with his thunderous snoring. My poor neighbors.

In my infinite wisdom, I gave him the benefit of the doubt and told myself he was just having a bad day. I was so wrong! A week later, he called me again on a Wednesday and asked me to come get him. Yes, I went and rescued him. (Maybe I should have invested in an ambulance and taken part in search-and-rescue as a profession. I think I missed my calling. It is what I am good at doing.)

When I arrived, he was holding a duffle bag and told me his truck was missing. I took him back to my condo and told him we would worry about it the next day. As I was helping him up the stairs, I felt a gun tucked in the back of his pants under his shirt. Great! Well, God prepared me (through the transition person from chapter two) for just such an occasion. Lucky me; it was a loaded .45 Smith & Wesson, the only gun I know how to use.

I took the clip loaded with bullets out and put it in a kitchen drawer. I hid the rest of the .45 in my linen closet under some towels. I then, freaking out, called my friend. I frantically told her that Romeo was already passed out with another sleeping pill up his nose and that I had the gun. She didn't help me. "What if he shot someone with it?" she said to me. So there I am, wiping my fingerprints off the gun with an imagined life sentence in jail passing in front of me. *What the hell was I doing?*

The next morning, I took him to work and started wondering how I was going to break it off. I said a little prayer. I asked God to give me discernment and strength.

God presented me with the opportunity the next day. That night, Romeo called me again to get him. That time it was the end. I found him with three other guys in the parking lot, in a car with the dome light on, doing cocaine. *Dumb!*

He tried to pull me into the car with him. I pulled him out of the car, gave him a kiss, and told him I loved him but that he was in God's hand now. I had a young child, and I did not want to be in jail. It hurt like hell to walk away from him yet again.

Romeo tried to get me to come back. I told him that my heart could not take it anymore. I asked him to never contact me again. The end. The end. The end. Finally. THE END.

Lesson Learned

God puts people back in our lives to show us what would have happened if we got what we thought we wanted and prayed for. God knows what is best for us (and I guess our parents do sometimes too). Unanswered prayers are some of God's greatest gifts!

And so I say, *"Next!"*

Praise God, See Me Naked

I met Bobby at a church I attended a while back, during a time when I was searching for a church to call home. Bobby was another person from the past, and although we never dated, we had known each other for years. One morning after the service, he asked me out for coffee. Given the fact that we were already familiar with one another, I went with no hesitation.

There is an expression you might or might have not heard: "radically saved Christian". Well, that was Bobby. This means he had strayed so far from God with his drug use, alcohol consumption, and gambling that now he was trying to be *too* good. Unfortunately, with him, there seemed to be no happy medium. It was all or nothing.

When people are new in a relationship, they tend to overlook things and rationalize away borderline behaviors. Well, that is what I did.

Over a period of three weeks, we met for dinners and some lunches. We prayed together, read the Bible, and had great conversation. Then, oh my goodness! As will be illustrated shortly, for some men, it only takes a few dates to show who they are.

I went to his house to meet up with him. I had to wait on the couch a few minutes because he had just come back from the gym and was not ready to leave when I arrived. Surprise! He said he would be just a minute and then we would go to dinner. He told me he was taking me out to a new Italian restaurant in the neighborhood.

As I am sitting there innocently watching the TV, I catch a glimpse of him out of the corner of my eye walking from the bedroom to the bathroom naked as a jaybird. Sitting there in disbelief, I was stunned that he actually had just done that, and it certainly seemed purposeful. I was not sure if I want to leave or stay. Unwisely, I talked myself into staying and worked hard to forget the whole incident and push it out of my mind.

Then he comes out wrapped tightly in a towel and asks if I think he needs to lose a little weight. I replied exasperatingly "Can you just get dressed? I am hungry!"

Now, you need to understand that he is a six-foot, blue-eyed, blond-haired (complete with ponytail) professional body builder with about a hundred and fifty pounds of muscle and seventy-five pounds of bones and flesh whom, I am sure, had tried that move before. He was divinely easy on the eyes, but I was not falling for the setup. He returned from the bedroom dressed and finally ready to go.

It was a balmy summer night, so we took his white special-edition Harley-Davidson motorcycle. We had a nice dinner and returned to his house to watch a movie. During the entire evening, there was absolutely no mention of the previous incident.

You will never guess what movie he picked out! *Left Behind*, the Christian movie, very popular at that time, about the end of times. I was still leery after all the things he pulled before dinner. We settled in on his black Italian leather couch to watch the movie. I told myself, *Maybe he was just testing my walk with the Lord.*

The next series of events that happened at the end of the movie forced the beginning of the end of our relationship. He got up and turned the movie off, put some sultry jazzy music, and lit some candles. He then aggressively moved on me with a tell-tale gleam in his eye.

I cringed. At that moment, I felt like I was in the lion's den and bracing myself to be devoured. He was staring ravenously into my eyes and pressed me with his strong hands. I then suddenly felt the pressure of all of his 225 pounds of flesh upon mine. The smell of his Giorgio cologne was also playing a part of the scary scene, as it was very overpowering. (Why do men have the "more is better" gene? Cologne is for a soft scent, not to bathe in it.) In a quiet whisper, he exhaled on me and said, "My flesh is weak."

Here we go! With great conviction and authority in my voice, I said, "Get your flesh off of me!" I stood up abruptly, fixed myself, and headed for the door. He foolishly asked if I would just stay and told me that he would be good if I would reconsider.

Oh, okay. As I said in chapter one, lesson learned. When people show you who they really are, believe them. I looked him in the eye and explained to him that I would send him a pair of my pants and he could get into them on his own time. I left with disgust. I have no communication with him anymore.

That was about the time I was getting mad at God for not giving me a break in my dating life. For a brief but powerful moment, I said to myself, *No more dating Italians or body builders!*

Unfortunately, I did not listen to my inner voice and suffered again, numerous times, with bad dates. Fortunately, though, it makes great book material, as you will read in the chapters to come. God was not yet done teaching me lessons. I was still operating in my own will, not God's. Sometimes we go around the mountain too many times because of our egos.

Lesson Learned

Date only in public, *and* neither men (nor women) should use God as a tool for hidden-agenda dating. By dating in public, there is less of a chance for inappropriate behavior from the prospective date. Meeting in public also gives you the chance to get up and leave if you are uncomfortable with the situation.

And so I say, *"Next!"*

The Latin Connection

I decided to join a salsa class and change it up a little. There is a saying that I am sure many have heard: "If you do what you always did, you get what you always got." Therefore, I tried salsa to see if I could affect my routine outcomes. As it turns out, I was a good student and enjoyed the activity and the distraction.

That was where I met Ricardo. Almost upon first introduction, he asked me to dance and moved me around the dance floor with ease. He was in his fifties and very distinguished, charming, and classically Latino. We danced, talked, and immediately connected on a comfortable level. Before we left the class, we exchanged phone numbers. We ended up meeting two days later for dinner. Things went surprisingly well, and we mutually decided to see each other again.

It seemed like this time the relationship was really going to go somewhere. Just about every weekend, he met me for dinner and dancing. Our interaction actually got to the point that we talked on the phone every night. I hoped that our growing affinity for one another might actually be something more permanent and turn into a good, healthy relationship. Wrong again!

One weekend, Ricardo and I went out with a larger group of people. One of the women took me aside and quietly asked if I knew his situation. I was puzzled and said that yes, we talked all the time. She did not elaborate any further, but it left me with an uneasy feeling. I did not confront him on the red flag right away. I decided to do my own investigating. Come to think of it, Ricardo would always meet me out and never forced himself on me or invited himself to my home. After all of what I had been through so far, I was just so happy that the friendship was progressing at a comfortable, slow pace. I did not think anything of it. However, in the back of my mind, I began to question. I am guessing God put the thought in my head. One random day, I decided to check his tax records. As in all municipalities, the county tax records are open to the public. I took a few moments to run his name, and there it was: Ricardo *and* Maria. It was time to confront him.

He called me that night to set a meeting place for our next dinner date. When he phoned, I asked him if he had a roommate. Ricardo said, matter-of-factly, yes, he did. I then asked if the roommate was his *wife*.

"Let me explain," he said concernedly. "My wife has two brain tumors, and I need love and affection."

Stunned, I took the time to enlighten him to the fact that it does not look good on a dating résumé if you are seeing other women while the one you love is dying. Really! And the poor woman had not one brain tumor, but two.

The thought of him parading me around to his friends while he was married completely unnerved me. I was disgusted and ashamed. What must his friends think of me? Ricardo actually said that they understood, but I did not. The last thing I asserted to him before I demanded that he never contact me again was, "I do not date married men!"

Lesson Learned

When exploring a possible relationship, ask specific, pointed questions (and do a county record check if you have to). People lie through omission of truth and information, my biggest pet peeve. Listen to your instincts; they are usually right. At times we tend to justify things we see because we don't want to be alone.

And so I say, *"Next!"*

Meet the Neighbors

My daughter (my family calls her "Sweet Face") was about eight years old when we moved in to my apartment. Because there were no young kids around, she amused herself in other ways. We lived on the second floor, and we had a balcony. She would sit out there after school and observe the neighbors while I made her a snack.

There was a man who taught karate who would come home the same time every day and wave to her. There was a woman in her eighties who was always working in her garden below us. Then there was Tony, who moved in with his daughter, Maggie, a few months later. Their balcony was right next to ours. My daughter was very fascinated by him.

He was a good-looking man who drove a black Fat Boy Harley. He had tattoos, and every day, out on the porch, he smoked and drank. Sweet Face was very intrigued by Tony. She must have been doing graphs that year in school because it was then that she thought she would start tally marks on how many cigarettes he smoked and when and how much beer he consumed daily. Paper and pen in hand, she would go sit on her little pink chair and watch him through the slats of the porch. After a few weeks, I asked what she was doing because it was always around 4:00 p.m. when she would go out there, like clockwork.

He would call her "Little One" and chitchat with her over the balcony, and they would do playful things like have squirt gun wars. Yes, he was a big kid and had a daughter, so, logically, we became friends. Maggie, who was fifteen, became like a big sister to my daughter. The four of us would go to dinner and swim at our pool together. Occasionally, we went to dinner or we would have them over for pizza and wings. The girls would play dress-up and have tea parties. It was so nice to see and be a part of their bonding.

One day while we were out together, we told him she did a graph on his smoking and drinking. He laughed with amusement and asked what the results were. She enlightened him to the fact that he smoked more Tuesday through Thursdays and, in addition, drank more beer on Fridays and Saturdays than any other days. She asked why that was. He laughed in amusement and said, "That is easy. I am paid on Fridays, and by Monday, I do not have any money left to drink, so I start smoking more because it is cheaper." Nice!

I eventually found out that Tony's wife had died of cancer two months before they moved in. I also learned that he was attempting to home school his daughter but became overwhelmed with the task. Therefore, when he finally sent her to public school for the first time, she was already in high school.

The other kicker was that they were Jehovah's Witnesses, worlds apart from what my beliefs are. Now, as a Witness, you are not allowed to smoke or drink, so the question in the not-so-back of my mind was exactly what he was doing partaking in both of those things.

We became close enough for him to eventually tell me that he was thrown out of the church because of his behavior after his wife died. His religion did not allow smoking, drinking, or tattoos, and he violated all those rules. It seemed his wife was everything to him, and he was having a tough time moving on. She was the one who kept him in line and on track with his life.

A few times we left our girls home and went out for dancing and for dinner. The subject of dating came up over dinner, and he confessed that he was having feelings for me. I told him I did not think the relationship could go anywhere. It was simple. I told him, "You are a fish, and I am a bird; they cannot live together." As you already have gathered, I am Christian and he is not, and our beliefs are extremely different. There is no middle ground between the two religions. He decided that from that point, it was a challenge, and *oh my, it became one.*

Over the months, Tony's drinking showed no signs of slowing down, and his daughter was getting worried. She called me one night and asked me to go get him at the bar. She was scared and wanted him home. I found him, helped him home, and walked him to the door. He looked in my eyes and, reeking of alcohol and slurring his words, told me, "Jules, I love you. Please be with me." Just then, Maggie opened the door, so the inevitable, uncomfortable conversation that would happen normally was interrupted. Thank goodness.

The next day, he told me that he remembered what he said to me the night before and meant it. I explained with as much kindness as I could muster that I would be his best friend but that I would not agree to date him. Tony was not happy with my response and tried to change it with a kiss. It would take more than a kiss to sway me at that point.

A few weeks passed, and then the trouble started. That time, when Maggie came home one night, he was gone, and she discovered that the phone book was open to "strip clubs." She called me and asked me for help. Yes, I found him and brought him back. I continued telling myself I was only doing it for Maggie. My heart was breaking for her. She had tragically lost her mother, and now she was also losing her father. How could I not help the poor child? I just thought of my own daughter and had to help.

Then, one Friday night at 2:00 a.m., I received a call from the sheriff's department. He had been arrested for DWI, and they wanted to know if I would come and pick him up. It is amazing to me (but I am sure only by the grace of God) that when these guys were in trouble, my daughter was always at her dad's house. I brought him home and told him very sternly that we would talk in the morning. *Maybe I should have bought that ambulance.*

Well, the next day, I told him I was done. I explained that he was disrupting my life and that I simply could not do it

J. Philippone

anymore. Sadly, and as one might expect, Tony was not happy with my bottom line and began a more self-destructive path.

Father's Day came, and there was a frantic knock at the door. It was Maggie. She was crying hysterically. I ran over to their apartment to find that Tony was facedown on the carpet, and I could not wake him up. Maggie called the ambulance as I instructed her to, and I proceeded to try to wake Tony. They rushed him to the local hospital and kept him for observation. He almost died of a lethal drug and alcohol combination.

When he came home from the hospital a few days later, I told him he really needed some rehab, and it helped that Maggie's grandparents pushed for it as well. They took her to live with them and would not let her return to live with him unless he was sober. While he was in rehab, we moved. I never saw him again. I pray for him and often wonder what happened to him and his daughter, but I know God has His hand on him wherever he is.

Lesson Learned

Do not rescue! Only date people who are at the same place in life as you are mentally, physically, and spiritually. Be confident in knowing that God will always provide a way out. It is our choice—our free will—to walk through that open door.

And so I say, *"Next!"*

There's a Full Moon Rising

There is something strange that happens when there is a full moon. People get crazy. People and their behaviors are very affected by the moon; I never noticed that until I was divorced.

Seemingly, out of the blue, I started getting phone calls at certain times of the month from the same gentleman. I use that word *gentleman* loosely. So I started keeping track of when certain calls started coming. Sure enough, about one to two days before the moon was full, like clockwork, they would dial me up. Each time they would call, they would pretty much say, "Jules, how ya doing? Just thinking about you." I explained to Sweet Face that any man who calls me "Jules" and wants to date me, I always say no. It kind of goes along with the full moon effect. They are usually contractors or salesmen and are *full of it*. I needed my boots on for the load of manure they were slinging at me.

One of the full moon men was Jimmy. Jimmy was a few years older than me, five feet ten inches tall, had blue captivating eyes, sandy-blond hair, was nicely built, and a great smile. Like the saying from the movie, when we first met, "He had me at hello." Initially, when he would speak, it was very mesmerizing. He had such great enthusiasm, and I couldn't help but be drawn in. Jimmy always had some new, exciting scheme that he wanted to tell me about. The reason for that, I found out, was that he wanted me to back him financially.

First, it was a billiard hall idea. He had a lathe with which he fixed pool cues at tournaments, and we went to Canada to work 9-ball tournaments. I have to admit, we did have a lot of fun meeting reporters from the Toronto Star and many top billiard players. His other ideas included a restaurant in Florida and starting a specialty chocolates shop. None of those things ever materialized.

Unfortunately for Jimmy, after the third or fourth full moon call, I had enough. I told him he was a dreamer, not a doer, and I was done with him. He pleaded his case and said we should get married because that would make things happen; we would be a power couple. Oh, okay.

I saw his daughter a few years later, and she told me he was living in Florida with some woman. Like I said before, when people show who they are, believe them.

Yet another one of the full moon men was Enrique from Cuba. We met at a local restaurant on the water during the summer. He happened to be about eight years younger than I was. He was dark skinned, six foot two, had dark eyes, and always smelled incredible. I love to salsa, so we began to go out and dance. Soon, we became friends.

One summer night, he came to pick me up wearing a white linen outfit. It was perfectly contrasted with his dark skin, and his smile would have knocked a plane out of the air. That evening, we danced at a local restaurant. When we went out on the patio, he was enjoying a cigar and told me that Tony from *Scarface* was his idol. Red flag!

That same night, he held me in his arms and, gazing into my eyes, said, "You are enough for me. Marry me." Then he told me he wanted me to go to Cuba with him to meet his parents so we could get married there. Maybe if I was born yesterday, his plan would have worked. I told him I did not see the relationship going anywhere permanent, especially because he wanted kids and I was done having them. He looked at me and said, "Is that your final answer?" Where were we, on *Who Wants to Be a Millionaire*?

Well, the romance ended, and he went away. But every time the moon was full, he would call and see if I had changed my mind and if we could get together. During one of the zany calls, he even offered to be my *pool boy*. I don't even have a pool! Clearly, he was looking for a sugar mama, and I was not going to be it. The last time I talked to him, he shared that he was living in Las Vegas, selling high-end clothes to rich women. That was perfect for him. I am sure he is someone's pool boy now.

Enter the last of the full moon men, Carlos. He was very entertaining but also a bit scary. He was a strapping, six-foot hunk of Italian and Spanish decent with dark skin and green eyes. His eyebrows were better than mine. A red flag should go up when you find out that a guy gets his eyebrows done. We met at a nightclub where he was a bouncer. He made pleasant conversation with me as soon as my friends and I walked through the door. He looked at me and said with a smile, "Carlos gets what Carlos wants." Why do people have to speak in the third person? I figured, *What the heck? Can't be any worse than what I have already experienced.*

Wrong! Carlos confided to me that he was a Navy SEAL but that I must not tell anyone. Then he informed me that he was just in town for a few weeks because his regular job was protecting an Israeli family in California. The question comes to mind, who was watching the family now? And it gets better. He had use of a van that he was borrowing from the people who owned the house where he lived in the basement. You might ask me, "Why didn't you run?" It is not as if I found this all out at once. That information gradually came out over a three-week period. It was at this point that I couldn't get rid of him. I was fortunate enough to have a Florida trip planned, and while I was gone, he found someone else to prey on. God gave me the open door, and I took it.

The experience with those three men (and some other contractors at work) was getting to be completely ridiculous. The full moon epidemic got so bad that I had to change my phone number. I have to admit that I was apprehensive to change it. What would I do without all the chaos? Have peace. What a concept.

Did I handle it? Instead of a New Year's resolution that year, I changed my cell number on January 1, and it was the best thing I ever did.

If you choose not to change your phone number, here is a little trick my friend told me about. If the men that you have determined are bad for you and in spite of you asking them not to still keep calling, change how you have them listed in your phone contact list. An example: If you know that *Joey Bag of Donuts* turned out to be a toad, when his number comes up, have it identify the caller as "*No Way!*" I did this for a person who was in my life, and it really makes me think, and it stops me from picking up the phone.

Lesson Learned

Do not answer the phone when the moon is full! If you do answer the phone, the "crazy" starts all over again. It is important to break the pattern or you will never get out of it. If you don't, as my friend Gary has said to me, you will feel like you are trying to rearrange the deck chairs on the Titanic…futile!

And so I say, "*Next!*"

Firemen and Policemen! Oh My!

During the next part of the journey, I seemed to attract men in uniform, specifically firemen and policemen. As we all know, they are in the field to rescue, so I figured, must be something in common, right? Wrong. They are looking for *someone* to rescue, and I didn't need to be rescued. That is not a challenge for them, but they keep coming back, and some have become part of the full moon epidemic that I have experienced.

I will start with the firemen and their *damsel in distress* syndrome. This particular fireman's name was Angelo, and he worked for the city. He was Italian, of course, six feet two inches tall, and had dark, dreamy, smiling eyes. Add to this equation the physique of a Roman soldier. Now you get the picture.

I was at local casual Italian restaurant with my girlfriends, and Angelo was there with his friends at the bar. The man locked eyes with me as soon as we were seated. When we finished dinner, the girls wanted to finish with a chocolate cosmopolitan at the bar, so we sauntered over. His eyes were still on me, and he was flashing me a terrific smile of his pearly whites. He sent over a drink, and the games began. We exchanged phone numbers, and he said he would call in the morning to set up a date. The way he expressed it was interesting: He said it was so we could have some "one-on-one time."

Angelo kept true to his word, and he called in the morning. We had a great conversation on the phone and made plans for that upcoming Friday night. He picked me up in his red Chevy Camaro. He also had a red Harley, a red speedboat, and a red 2500-HD Chevy truck. I got it; he liked red because he was a fireman.

At any rate, we went to a nice Italian restaurant and continued to learn about each other. We both had been married before and were looking for the same thing out of a relationship: love, commitment, and trust. He failed to tell me at that time he also needed *someone to rescue.*

There are actually many positive examples of this tendency. Angelo was nice enough to climb the tree in my backyard and install a tire swing for my daughter. She was thrilled and, to this day, still plays on it with her friends. He also fixed a light in my yard and my dishwasher and changed the oil in my vehicle. Angelo also let me borrow his truck while mine was in the shop so I would be able to get my daughter from school one afternoon. Nevertheless, that was not needy enough for him.

After a few weeks, the independence he was attracted to in me turned into frustration for him. Why? He felt like I didn't need him. In one of our conversations, he expressed that I had a good job, vehicles that ran well, and I have a daughter and my own house, so why did I need him? I explained that I would think he would be happy that I am not a needy, jealous, or controlling woman. Over much debate, he decided that he wanted to end our relationship. In a last attempt at half-kidding, half-serious humor, I suggested that I be the damsel in distress every few weeks and he could save me on the side of the road. He was not amused, and that was where it ended.

The two policemen I encountered were as equally entertaining with their views on relationships. The first was a lieutenant in one of the local suburbs who lived part time in both Rochester and in Syracuse. Whenever we spoke about his situation and I asked why, I never really got the full answer from him. I know for sure he wasn't married and had a daughter in college in Rochester.

Lieutenant Vinny, as I liked to call him, was about five feet ten inches tall with sandy-brown hair and brown eyes. The lieutenant was always impeccably dressed and wore Armani cologne that drove me wild. He had a great smile and always said the right thing in every situation. Our conversations were very flirty and witty, and I could see his amusement in me when we spoke. At one point, I said to him that I felt like the female version of him. He was greatly intrigued after that conversation. The best way to describe our repartees is to liken it to a scene from *His Girl Friday* with Cary Grant and Rosalind Russell.

We dated for about a month, just dinner and coffee here and there because he would travel between Syracuse and Rochester. I believe he started getting a little too attached to me and, as a result, started breaking dates with a questionable story every time. For example, one of the stories was he had to cancel because he was cutting the lawn and a group of ground bees attacked him. Another was he was on a high-profile stakeout and couldn't get away. Interesting. I pay attention to details, and I knew his schedule. I knew it was one of his days off.

On a few occasions, I conducted a damsel in distress test of my own, and I was right. I needed a ride because my car broke down, so I called, and guess what. He was there in twenty minutes, no questions asked or excuses for not being around. I tried it again a week later. I needed a ride to the airport and called him at the last minute, and sure enough, he was there to rescue me.

In conclusion, he, like the others, was not interested in me unless I needed rescuing. We are still friends, and I always laugh when he calls around the full moon. He wants to see how I am doing and says we will "get together soon." I do not hold my breath. I wrote this book.

The next person was a sheriff who was a friend of a friend who thought we would be perfect together. His name was

Paulie, and he was about forty-five years old, six feet tall, and had hazel eyes. On our first date, we went to a restaurant where he sat in the booth with his back to the wall so he could see the front door (I have noticed this habit when I was out with another police officer). Before I even had my salad, he started talking about marriage. I almost choked when he said, "I only date Italian women with the intention of marriage and three children." Well, what do you say after that? I informed him we might not like each other after dessert so perhaps he should consider slowing it down. During the conversation, he informed me had been married twice already with no kids from both marriage and asked if I still wanted kids. I said, "If God wants it to be so, I will have them."

That naturally brought us on to the next question, which was about God and religion. Paulie explained to me that he believed in God but also that God controls the aliens. *Check please!* Thank goodness I drove myself to dinner; I couldn't get out of there fast enough. All I could picture was him looking for alien ships on his night shift.

The definition of *normal* is very broad. What is normal to one is not to another, so I gave up on guessing what is normal for those men I was encountering.

In my frustration, after most of these dates, I would call my cousin Ann Marie. She has always been like a sister to me growing up and to this day. Her words of wisdom always make me laugh. She would always say to me with great conviction, "Jul, don't worry. Just put another tombstone in the backyard with the dummy's name on it!"

Lesson Learned

If you are a strong woman, *don't compromise* to be a damsel in distress; you will hate yourself later for settling. The more lessons I learned, the smarter I was in my dating life, and the stronger I became.

And so I say, *"Next!"*

Do You Yahoo?

After all of this, you might be wondering this about me: *What kind of dating hasn't she tried at this point?* I have even tried Internet dating. It is a sport within itself.

When the Internet sites started popping up for dating, I thought, *Why not?* So I took my picture and put it out there for the world to see. Big mistake! People misrepresent themselves with fifteen-year-old pictures and fake jobs and loving to take long walks on the beach. Give me a break, guys! Just be honest!

It was so frustrating. I finally posted this disclaimer in my profile: "If you live with your mother, don't have a car or a job, and can't balance your checkbook, *do not* bother me!" My ex-husband actually searched me on the Internet and told me my profile was too brutal and I would never get a man that way. With your knowledge of the last eight chapters, I will leave it to your imagination exactly what I said to him.

Needless to say, the idiots still kept e-mailing me. I found it entertaining until such point that I didn't anymore. I found men with four kids living with their mothers and needing a place to live. There was also a forty-five-year-old man who lived in the country in the garage where he fixed cars and had a black widow spider as a pet. He informed me that if I came to visit him, be prepared—he had no running water to his garage. A "renaissance man" is what he called himself. He had a fully restored 1961 Porsche but no plumbing in his garage (priorities)? So if I visited, he said he would give me a bucket if I needed to use the bathroom. *What a gentleman!*

And then there was Joe, a fifty-year-old Italian male, never married, living in the same house and room since he came over from Italy when he was ten. His defense was, "Why move? I get food prepared when I want it, and my clothes are washed and folded." I have to tell you, he was six feet tall, always tan, in great shape, and oozing with testosterone. I heard women at the gym say they wouldn't mind having his boots under their bed. Joe also had two nice high-profile vehicles and always had a roll of money in his pocket.

Just for entertainment, I went out with him a few times. Joe behaved as a gentleman, and except for a kiss, nothing physical happened between us. I am sure he didn't understand why, after two dates, we weren't sleeping together, because he could clearly have anyone he wanted. So when I said *enough,* he left me with an interesting proposition. I know you will find it as hard to believe as I did, but this is yet another example of why I was compelled to write this book. The truth is crazier than fiction.

On a moonlit night in July, we were parked in his black Corvette with the top down, sitting in my driveway. I was telling him the relationship wasn't going anywhere but that I felt like we could be friends. Joe took my hands and looked into my eyes. He explained to me that if I got lonely, just for *me*, he would come when I called. He reminded me that he played cards with the boys near my house on Fridays, so he would be in the neighborhood. All I would have to do was answer the door in my robe and he would "take care of me" and go to his game afterward. What a nice guy (sarcasm). I wonder how many other women he is "taking care of." *So not worth it!*

If you choose to date on the Internet, be sure to be safe; tell a friend who he is, his phone number, and where you are meeting. Don't let him meet you at a shopping mall or thruway stop; make the date at a location that is comfortable for you, such as a popular restaurant in your own area. It does not hurt if you plant some friends at the restaurant in a booth near you. In this day and age, you can find out a lot just by a Google search of his name, and I encourage you to do that.

Lesson Learned

For many men, online dating is a sport. I have found that you cannot date online and find a substantial relationship. God managed to put people together just fine without the Internet for thousands of years. I am confident that I am one day closer to the man-of-God that will eventually be in my life.

And so I say, *"Next!"*

My Consigliores

Consigliore is an Italian word for "advisor." I am fortunate to have two: Vito and Luigi. Both of them are twenty years my senior and own their own businesses. They have become my angels. They look exactly like they sound, with salt-and-pepper hair slicked back nicely with gold chains and pinkie rings. Surprisingly, they have never asked me to kiss the ring. (If you're not Italian or you did not see *The Godfather*, you might not understand. Ask someone who did.) Vito drives a pearl-white Cadillac Escalade, and Luigi drives a black Lincoln Town Car. They watch out for me in business and matters of the heart. I come to them when I need guidance and a safe place to talk about either topic. Being with them is like the old saying about being in Vegas—what you see and say stays with them. Nice!

If I am in need of advice or just having a bad day, I find out where they are, and we have "a meeting." That is our secret code for where they are going so no one can find them. I will call Vito and ask where the meeting is, and he says, "Hey, kid. You need a little advice today? The meeting will be at the eastside location at 5:30 p.m. See you then!" I always feel like I am in a scene from an Italian movie like *Analyze This* with Robert De Niro.

They are so funny with their advice. I am laughing thinking of them right now. They always pick out-of-the-way places that are "joints," not chain restaurants where everyone potentially knows them. They like to sit and play the numbers to pass the time. If I help pick the numbers and they win, I get half. Such a deal! Vito will be sitting on one side of me, and Luigi will stand on the other side. They intently listen to my tale of the day and, with me in the middle, discuss it.

At one particular "meeting," I was concerned about a man I had been dating named Enzo. My gut had been telling me, "No good for you," so I decided to talk to my consigliores about it. I love them! It went like this:

Vito said, "What do you think of this guy she is dating, Luigi?"

Luigi said, "No good. I think we should check on him."

Vito said, "I agree." He then looked at me and said. "Okay, kid. This is what I am going to do. I know a guy who knows your new love, so let me make a call tomorrow, and then you can make the right decision."

How could I say no? I agreed not to see Enzo again until Vito called me with the green light.

It took two days for Vito to call me back, so I began to get worried. I knew in my gut what the answer was going to be. It is my experience that if you have to ask someone what not to do, you shouldn't be doing it.

Vito called and said, "Okay, kid. Are you gonna listen to what I have to say or not?"

I told him I would or I wouldn't have asked. He asked me if I was emotionally invested. I asked why, and he said, "Run like a bunny, honey!" I had to ask again why, and Vito explained that my new love interest had a "pony problem" (gambling) and a drug habit. Oh yeah! Another winner!

Therefore, I ended it by telling Enzo that we were in different places in our lives because his kids were grown and I still had a grammar school child. He fought it a little, but amazingly, we parted with no incidents.

I not only had my consigliore, I also had my daughter's godfather to talk to about these crazy men. After all these dating experiences, I would call and tell of their shenanigans, and he would say to me, "Again, I apologize for the male population!"

My girlfriend Sue still says to this day she doesn't know what scares her most, the men I meet or the people who check them out for me.

Lesson Learned

Ladies, it is always good to have a consigliore or two. They don't have to be Italian, just someone that acts as your guardian angel on earth.

And so I say, *"Next!"*

J. Philippone

Why Do I Feel Like I Have Been Here Before?

At this point, you are probably asking yourself, *Hasn't she learned enough lessons? Can't she see things coming, or is she still blind to these men and their shenanigans?*

I went through so much turmoil with dating that I could easily write another book, but I do not know if that will happen. Many women have been through things that have hardened their hearts to men. I did not want to be one of them, so I took these experiences and looked at them like blessings in disguise.

I met Antonio years ago, when he was first starting in the roofing business, well before he owned his company. I knew he was Christian and went to church with his mom every week. He walked into my office looking for business on the property I managed. That is where we met for the first time.

Antonio asked for my number and asked me if we could have dinner sometime. I agreed to dinner, and we made plans to make it happen. He was about five feet ten inches tall, with dark hair that was a perfect metrosexual style. He had green eyes with long eyelashes. I had never seen him without a tan either.

We met at the restaurant because, after all my bad experiences, I did not want to be stuck in a tough situation. I was there first and was waiting when a red Ferrari convertible with the top down pulled up in front of me. Antonio was wearing nice-fitting jeans and a green shirt that perfectly matched his eyes. He asked for a quiet table in the back of the restaurant.

We drank a bottle of wine with dinner and caught up on what we had been doing for the last ten years. Divorce and kids were the main topic for the first part of our conversation, followed by what we were currently looking for in a relationship. Things were going well, and I felt comfortable with the way the evening was going, so we went back to his house. I had been there before when his parents owned the house and did not feel a bit of concern about going back. *Just in case*, I followed him to his house. I'm so glad I did.

He lived on a street where the all the houses are brick and were built in the early 1900s. Most of the places had Mercedeses, BMWs, and Lexuses parked in the driveways. Every home on the street was immaculately landscaped.

We arrived at his house and entered through the front door. On the right was the living room with the huge-screen TV and the black leather Italian sofa. Big surprise! The kitchen was beautiful with cherry wood cabinets and granite counters, complete with an island in the middle—a kitchen from every woman's dreams.

He proceeded to show me the way upstairs to see the kids' rooms and his room. I wish I had pictures of his bedroom to put in this book. Let me try to describe it: The "love nest" was at least twenty feet by twenty feet with four bordello red walls. In the center, against the wall, was a round bed with black satin covers. Hung suggestively over the bed was a chandelier. There were also half-melted candles and massage oil on a nightstand. There were mirrors on the ceiling and leopard sheets on the bed. There was even a gold statue in the corner of the room. On the wall for watching from the bed, let us not forget, was a plasma TV with a DVD player attached. I can only imagine with that setup what kind of DVD collection he had. Okay. So around that time, I was thinking, *Now what?* and the sick feeling was growing in my stomach: *Get out!*

I excused myself to go downstairs to get a drink of water. He followed me and began making his moves. While I was drinking the water at the sink, he came at me from behind and started kissing my neck. I slowly turned and looked into his eyes and said, "Okay. Let's have a little chat."

I explained to him that one does not build a house and put the roof on first; the foundation is built, and then the walls, and finally the roof. I told him to think about my comments while I use the little girls' room. Well, he thought about it, but nothing about what I said. He called to me from his room and asked me to come upstairs to see him. With great hesitation, I slowly entered the room. He was, in PG-rating description, on his bed, posing for me with nothing on but a smile. I felt like I was in a bad B movie—a really bad B movie.

I was so mad I could not see straight. He actually said to me, "Just because you want to be good does not mean that I have to be." A nice Christian man with good morals!

I wondered if his churchgoing mother would approve of that behavior. I told him that I did not know whom he had dated before but that was unacceptable behavior in *my* book and to go ahead without me and have a nice life. Thank God I drove myself there.

Then there was Luke, a man I knew from years ago. I worked with him at one of my first property management jobs. We reconnected one summer night while I was listening to a band at a local club in town with my girlfriends. We did not make it the first time because he was just sober and going through AA. We parted on good terms and as friends but lost touch for many years.

Luke is a few years older than I am, with two adult children and recently divorced. He was a slender six-foot-two-inch tall man with blond hair and a small gold hoop earring in his right ear. He also had a flame tattoo on his arm that matched the flames on his white Fat Boy Harley he rode. Interesting! We caught up on old times and, after a bit of conversation, thought we should give our relationship another chance. For a while, things were going well, and he invited me to drive down to bike week in Daytona, Florida, with him and his friend James. By this time, we had been seeing each other casually for four months. I decided *Why not?* because we were going with a third person, his friend James. James also knew my family, so I felt safe.

Luke, James, and I were taking our journey in a white Chevy Tahoe with a trailer towed behind it for the bikes. They were taking along their motorcycles and some other friends' rides because they were flying down. I was recovering from bronchitis, and he was a smoker, so the ride down was tough. Luke would not stop smoking, and I was coughing to the point of gagging. He actually told me to suck it up. Then James told him he should be more respectful. It fell on deaf ears. I could see at this point that I might have made a wrong decision. Going away with someone has a tendency to open up your eyes. He also shared that he decided he was going to cleanse his colon while we drove down with green aloe drinks and power drinks in between.

We stopped for the night and had a room with two beds. The two guys were in one, and I was in the other. The next morning, Luke's aloe drink kicked in and, oh my gosh, his friend James and I had to leave the room. Nasty! Luke thought it was all very amusing that he ran us out. I did not share his sense of humor on the matter.

James's daughter lived in South Carolina, so we arrived there the next day and stayed the night. I was not feeling well, so I lay down. Luke stormed in the room and informed me that if I was going to ride his Harley, I better get out there and wash it. *Are you kidding me?* James witnessed the scene and asked me what the heck I was doing with him. I informed him that my eyes were now open and I would leave and go home if it got to be too much.

I did not wash his bike, but he took me for a ride anyway. I asked him to take it easy because he did not know the area. Luke had selective hearing and went 80 mph on the highway. I was on the back of that Harley, making deals with God. We finally stopped at the Harley store, and he bought me a shirt. Gratefully, James happened to be there with the truck, so I rode home with him. With much dismay, Luke went back by himself. We all went out to a casual local Mexican restaurant. As we ate dinner, I was getting the cold shoulder treatment from Luke. We got home, and James's daughter said she would drive me to the airport. She knew I needed to get away from Luke. At that point, I agreed.

The next morning, I got up, packed, and headed to the door, but not without another confrontation. It felt like I was more drained in four days from this person than during my entire marriage. We got to the airport. He kept making comments about the plane going down and that I had better say a prayer. It was just plain abusive behavior. It felt like I was just getting off Mr. Toad's Wild Ride at Disney. Luke was not the same man from New York. I do not know what happened. On the plane, I was an emotional wreck and still physically sick. I called my parents and told them I needed to be picked up from the airport and I would explain when I got home. The end!

Lesson Learned

Do not recycle men in your life. As has been said, if you keep doing what you always did, you keep getting what you always got: aggravation and unacceptable male behavior.

And so I say, *"Next!"*

The Country Player

At some point, I decided to try something different. My girlfriend wanted to learn how to line dance, so I figured that would be an interesting change. After all, I have tried salsa. Why not line dance? We went to a local country bar and took in the atmosphere. The women were in their painted-on jeans and tight shirts, the men in their cowboy hats and tight jeans and snakeskin boots. The whole place looked like a rustic-type barn with heavy beams of timber, and the tables and chairs were made of rough wood. Everyone was having fun and was quite friendly.

My friend Sue and I sat down to rest and have a drink at the bar. It was then that a nice, handsome man in a cowboy hat strolled over. He was six feet tall with dark hair and a kind face that was smiling at me. The jeans he was wearing fit him nicely, and he had on the cologne Diesel. He introduced himself as Cody, and he and his friend asked if we would like to dance. We explained that we were beginners. Cody said he would be "gentle with us" and would love to teach us a few moves. I'll bet!

We had a great time, and we exchanged phone numbers so that we might meet for dinner the following week. He was not from the area and lived in farm country about thirty minutes away. So we decide to meet halfway between for dinner. Cody and I had a few dates, and then he invited me out to his place for an afternoon to go four-wheeling. When we first met, we had a pleasant conversation about things we both like to do, and that was one of them.

I arrived at his house. It was an old white farmhouse with acreage behind it. His brand-new black Chevy one-ton pickup was parked in the driveway. This truck was lifted to the point where he had to help me into it.

On the acreage was an ostrich farm. It was the strangest thing to see in person. He offered me one of the eggs to give to Sweet Face, so I willingly accepted. (I still have it to this day.) Cody and I went to his garage before he showed me the rest of the house. When he opened that door, my mouth dropped open. It was something from a magazine.

The garage was worth more than the house. I am sure of it. It was something a NASCAR driver would have at their home. The floor was custom, complete with a drain and a lift to work on vehicles. Diamond plate was everywhere, and all the helmets for every sport were lined up, complete with the outfit that went with them. Cody had two snowmobiles, two ATV four-wheelers, racing motorcycles, and a 1970 black fully restored Mustang covered in the corner. I was impressed.

Cody helped me into his Chevy truck, and we went to get something to eat at a local pizza place where everyone knew him. Then we headed back to the house to four-wheel on his property. I thought I would get to use my own ATV, but he wanted me on the back of his. He took me for a tour of his property and that of his family, which was conveniently across the street from him. Apparently, they had a hundred acres that was used for dairy farming. The sun was starting to set, and we headed back to his house.

Cody said he wanted to give me the rest of the tour of his house. I was expecting it to look like the garage, but it did not. It was a typical old farmhouse, true in nature with the country kitchen, hardwood floors, and a fireplace in the living room. He invited me upstairs to see his computer room and bedroom.

Well, the upstairs was more like the garage caliber than the first floor of the house. There was a wall of recording equipment on one side. The other side had a computer and some other electric equipment I had never seen, complete with a leather couch. I knew it had to be somewhere. What is it with these guys and the leather couches? Oh, and I forgot to mention that he was also Italian. I know. I really have to break this pattern.

On with the story. He said he had all this equipment because he did websites and recorded jingles for commercials. After we talked for about an hour, he said he wanted to show me his hangout/bedroom where he spent the rest of his time. My thoughts were, *Hold on to your seats. It's going to be a bumpy ride!* Well, by now, you know it is going to be bad or I would not be including him in this book. How many guys in the world does this cheesy bedroom setup work for? It must work a lot because they keep doing it.

So I enter the hangout/bedroom and I am not disappointed in my educated expectation; it is exactly what I expected. He must have pulled a page right out of *Playboy* magazine. There was, on the left, some Boticelli art and a wall with a sixty-inch TV with complete surround sound. The back wall had two red chairs on either side of the window that looked like they came from the movie *Austin Powers*. Then there was the California king bed complete with satin sheets and a nightstand with half-melted candles and a half-empty bottle of massage oil. And to my right, in the corner of the room, there was a hot tub. As I was taking all this in, he looked at me, smiled, and said, "It's all good, baby, right?" I felt like the Christians at the Coliseum, ready to be devoured.

Before I had time to answer, my phone rang. It was my ex-husband. My daughter was sick, and I needed to get back because she was calling for me. I explained this to Cody and thanked God all the way home for giving me a way out. As you might remember from the beginning of this book, I ask God for discernment whenever I go on a date, and he gives it to me pretty quickly. Sometimes the answers feel like lightning bolts hitting me.

Cody called me later to see how my daughter was doing. I told him everything was fine and I did not think we would work because we lived so far apart. Well, much to my surprise, he agreed. He then told me that after I left that he got a phone call, and it was from the girl he broke up with two months before, and she was pregnant. Imagine that. Therefore, he said he did not know what he was going to do and he would see me "around."

Lesson Learned

Do not get "played" by the players; they do not just live in the big city. Look for warning signs as illustrated in this chapter (candles, massage oil, hut tub, the lair!). Remember, those who become aware then need to be responsible.

And so I say, *"Next!"*

J. Philippone

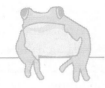

"E" Sensei

I saved this person for chapter thirteen. You will see why. It is just plain amusing. It is amazing how so many men think women are stupid. As long as they dress well, smell good, and flash their pearly whites, they can feed us any line and we will swoon for them. Not *this* woman!

I am laughing as I remember this story about my daughter's karate teacher. Sweet Face was in karate for four years. Our neighbor owned the studio and offered free lessons to see if she would like it. Karate turned out to be very good for her, so we were there until she decided to start volleyball, which she still plays to this day.

All the parents would sit in the front of the studio near the entrance door. The mirror and mats were in the rest of the studio. It was nice to talk to other moms to pass the time. As people came in, they would have to walk in front of the parents to reach the mats. One of the instructors was Italian and Spanish (again, I know, I know; I have not learned the lesson enough). Franco was six feet three inches tall and bronze with long hair tamed in a ponytail. He was about seven years younger than me. *Adonis*, ladies. Adonis.

A month of our flirting with our eyes went by with no words exchanged. Then he finally said hello and we conversed about my daughter and how well she was doing. He asked about her dad. I explained that Sweet Face's father and I were divorced and that I was single.

The next week, he had enough nerve to ask me for my number. He wanted to know if we could have coffee and get to know each other. Franco was quick to call me that Tuesday night, and while we were out, we had a great conversation. He told me that he was a physical therapist and donated time to help cancer patients, and I thought, *Hmm. Nice…maybe.* No red flags either. We met for coffee again the next day, and all went well. We talked and flirted heavily.

Franco asked if I would like to meet for dinner that Friday night. I said yes, of course. I was intrigued.

He picked me up in his black Chevy Corvette. Go figure! Franco came to my door and escorted me to the car, opened my door, and helped me in. He had soulful jazz playing, and the car smelled of his fabulous cologne. He was dressed in a white linen shirt and pants that complemented his skin perfectly. He looked like he just walked off the cover of a romance novel.

We went to the lake and had dinner by the water. It was a perfect summer night. The sun was setting, and the waves were softly rolling in. I knew there was going to be a full moon that night.

The light of the moon should have been a spotlight on him saying, "Danger Ahead!" Franco ordered a bottle of wine, and we had a toast to our new beginnings. We finished dinner and walked in the moonlight, where we had our first kiss near the beach. This was a kiss that you could feel to your toes. I was truly hoping this could be a solid relationship. Things were looking up until, suddenly, they were not.

Over the phone a few nights later, he turned into this person that I just could not believe. His comfort level with me must have been high, and he was working his "A" game on me, which must have worked in the past with other women. It went something like this: He bragged, "You know, I used to live in New York City and was a bouncer at a club. Girls would get in free if they helped me out."

I said, "Helped you out?"

In a matter-of-fact manner, he replied, "Yes, I would let them in for free, and they would go in the bathroom and take care of me," he said with a devilish laugh.

Is he really telling me this? I replied with an attempt to change the subject that I was not going there with him.

Then he proceeded to tell me that he had size thirteen feet, hinting at what he hoped to be obvious.

I said, "Must be hard to find shoes." I was not giving him the satisfaction of that conversation.

Franco then pushed again. "You know *why* I am telling you this?"

"Because your birthday is coming up and you want me to buy you some new sneakers?" I quipped with serious tone in my voice.

He was greatly frustrated with me and gave up and said good night.

The next time I saw Franco at the karate studio, it was a little bit awkward. He just smiled at me and walked away. I never did hear from him again. Then my daughter started volleyball soon after, thank God.

So now you know why this is chapter thirteen!

Lesson Learned

Someone once said that you get what you tolerate. Ladies, do not tolerate bad behavior. (I know I am repeating myself because we *all* need to get it.) Think more of yourselves and you will find healthier dates. Stay true to your core values.

And so I say, *"Next!"*

How It Ends, Only God Knows

I thought by the time I finished this book I would be married for sure. I am not. What have I learned by all these experiences is that marriage is not for everyone. Sometimes God just wants us to rely on Him, not a human being. He enables us to have the peace and direction we need in our lives. The company would be nice but is not essential. All we have to do is ask Him in our hearts to lead and direct us. We have to be quiet enough to hear from Him.

When I do, it is not an audible voice I hear; it is a thought, a nuance, or something I read. If I had not asked and prayed for God's gift of discernment every time I went on a date, I would not be where I am today. By this point, I would have compromised for sure. Compromise should not occur because we feel stuck or as if the present man in our life is our *last chance* for happiness. I would rather honor my core values and potentially be alone than go through what I have depicted in this book. A good rule of thumb I learned is if I wouldn't let them date my daughter, I shouldn't be dating them.

One of the things I did during this journey is to find a life verse for myself to live by to be an example to my daughter. It took me about six months to find the right one, and I did. It is Proverbs 31:25-28 (NASB):

> Strength and dignity are her clothing and she smiles at the future. She opens her mouth in wisdom, and the teaching of kindness is on her tongue. She looks well to the ways of her household, and does not eat the bread of idleness. Her children rise up and bless her...

These are the characteristics of a virtuous woman, which I strive to be.

The other thing that happened over the last ten years was the rekindling of my relationship with my mother. Every morning, I talk with my mother. Ours is a relationship I cherish at this time in my life. We did not always understand each other as we do now. I am grateful for her love and friendship. She would always ask me how any given each relationship was going and if they were at the "curb" yet. It was a private joke we shared; trash day is Thursdays at my house. We would both laugh and she would chime in with her special brand of humor, "Next!" Thus, the title of the book emerged.

A question my mother posed to me one morning helped me come to an insightful observation. She asked me if anyone of the men of trash day was married yet. Guess what. None of them are. What does this mean? I have no idea, but it was an intriguing fact to ponder. When I thought about it, I did know why. Those men are, for the most part, emotionally messed up, unavailable, or both.

My mother started telling me to look up and find my prince, not down at the wounded birds. Leave them alone! Good advice.

It is comforting to now know that I do not have to rush into a relationship or marriage. God is the only man in my life. He will not leave me. He will not forsake me. It's true that He cannot hug me, but I have great friends and family that will.

The moral of my stories: enjoy life and do not feel guilty for wanting to. There is nothing wrong with you if you are single. It is a lie we tell ourselves. Others love to help us feel that we are less than, if we let them. I choose to disregard negative people and filter them out of my life.

I will say it again. We have choices! Be a blessing going into a room and a blessing going out. When you make an appearance, be the person that people want to talk with, not run from. Each new day is a present from God, so enjoy the journey of life.

Lesson Learned

You do not need to see to believe good things will happen in your life; just be positive and know you and God are a majority.

And so I say, *"Next!"*

Finally, with great expectation, on my way to Italy with my daughter for two weeks!

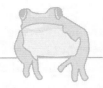

Success

Recently, when I was sitting on the airplane on my way to Rome, Italy, while looking at my sweet daughter next to me, I had a smile on my face and joy in my heart. I was reviewing the last ten years of being a single mom and realized that, gratefully, God was the bulldozer in front of me and the janitor behind me. I am a better woman-of-God than I was when I started writing this book. As a result of this journey, I have had success with picking better dates and attracting healthier people. I have a solid relationship with my daughter with no craziness—just peace and direction.

Women, our children are watching us. They are looking for direction not by what we say but what we do. One of my friends told me about *Passport to Purity* by Dennis and Barbara Rainey and encouraged me to listen to it with my daughter. I strongly encourage every mom to listen to it with their daughter or son. At the end, it asks the child to make a *purity promise*. I did this right before my daughter entered high school so she would make wise decisions. We both made the *purity promise*—which has been a great success. The *purity promise* means putting God first place in your heart and maintaining moral purity. My daughter is graduating this year and has made wonderful choices and smart decisions. It will be the hardest thing you do with your child but the biggest blessing also.

If I would have been out every night drinking or bringing different men home every month, Sweet Face would not be the woman-of-God she is today. We have a "peace that passes all" in our home. In ten years, my daughter only met three men that I thought might have gone somewhere with a relationship. When the relationships ended, I would explain why. The main reason was because we were not equal in our beliefs.

I cannot preach one path to my daughter and live another. During this time I realized I *wanted* to be single to enjoy the short window of opportunity to spend with my daughter before she went to college. The days that I might have felt lonely I would pray for God to satisfy my soul for that one day, and I still do that to this day. I would then ask Him to show me if there was an area in my life that needed work. The answer came: "clean your house" and all areas of your life. I am an organized person by nature, but what it meant to me was get the clutter out of my life—like the toads in my life. So I am happy to say that my car, house, and office at work have no clutter. It was a process, for sure, but it kept me busy on those Friday and Saturday nights when I was home alone. It was then that I also started eating healthier and exercising on a regular basis. I had restored *balance* to my life. Amen!

Another success was that I was introduced to a great man but learned from experience he would not be a good match for me but for someone else. So I introduced him to my girl-friend. They met and dated for a few years—I went to their wedding recently. They are happy and a perfect match. I have heard people are in our lives for a reason, season, or a lifetime. That made me realize I had to introduce the two of them. This has been the only match I have made, but it was definitely under God's watchful eye. (They're both devout Christians.)

Every time I met a new man, I would stop writing this book and put it in a box in the back of my closet. I would think to myself, *Maybe he is the one and I do not need to finish the book.* Wrong! How many things do we have in the back of our closets or our minds that gnaw and prod at us that we should finish? Don't let other people, as well as your mind, tell you it's impossible. Remember—*you* and God are a majority. He wants you to lean on Him, as well as rely on yourself. My mother said to me for years, "*Pull yourself up by your pantyhose and get your butt out there!*" If we don't make a step of faith, He can't help us.

I am grateful that God has kept me single—which is a definite statement I never thought would ever come out of my mouth! This incredible journey has enabled me to finish this book without distraction and be a good example to my daughter.

Many preachers say, "It's not how you start; it's how you finish," and I am finishing happy, content, and strong!

Contact Information

For more information about *And So I Say, "Next!"* and author Julie Philippone, please visit her Facebook page at www.facebook.com/andsoisaynext1.